ANIMAL TRACKERS
AROUND THE WORLD

AT THE POLES

Tessa Paul

CRABTREE
Publishing Company

CRABTREE
Publishing Company

350 Fifth Avenue	360 York Road, R.R.4	73 Lime Walk
Suite 3308	Niagara-on-the-Lake	Headington, Oxford
New York, NY 10118	Ontario LOS IJO	England OX3 7AD

Editor **Greg Nickles**
Designer **Janelle Barker**
Consultant **Karen Jane Kemmis-Betty (M.Sc.)**

Illustrations
Andrew Beckett (cover background, track marks)
All other illustrations courtesy of Marshall Cavendish Partworks: Robin Boutell/WLAA (page 16);
Robin Budden/WLAA (pages 24-25); John Cox/WLAA (pages 11, 13, 24, 30-31); Barry Croucher/WLAA
(page 11); Mark Donnelly/WLAA (pages 8, 9, 10); Lee Gibbons/WLAA (page 17); Ruth Grewcock (page 15);
Steve Kingston (pages 4-5, 30); Peter David Scott/WLAA (page 14); Richard Tibbitts (pages 28-29);
Simon Turvey (page 13)

First printed 1998
Copyright © 1998 Crabtree Publishing Company

Cataloging-in-Publication Data

Paul, Tessa

At the poles / Tessa Paul
p. cm — (Animal trackers)
Includes index.
ISBN 0-86505-590-4 (library bound)   ISBN 0-86505-598-X (pbk.)
Summary: Introduces the physical characteristics, behavior, and tracks of animals that live
at the North or South Poles, including the polar bear, seal, and penguin.
1. Zoology—Polar regions—Juvenile literature. [1. Zoology—Polar regions. 2. Animal tracks.]
I. Title. II. Series: Paul, Tessa. Animal trackers.
QL104.P38 1998   j591.7'0911   LC 98-10864
CIP

CONTENTS

AT THE POLES

Everyone knows that
the world is icy and frozen
around the North and South
Poles. There is, however, more
than just ice in these regions.
There is a large amount of
land around both poles.

In the north, inside of the Arctic
Circle, is the land called the tundra.
The tundra is flat and rocky, and
it is not always covered completely
in snow. Around the South Pole,
inside of the Antarctic Circle,
are the icy continent of Antarctica
and many rocky islands.

At both poles,
spring and summer
bring a great change
to the cold landscape.
Blossoms and grass bloom
on the tundra, and thousands
of birds come to nest. Northern and southern
seas warm up, swarming with fish and other
sea life. Whales migrate to both polar regions.

This book tells you
how these and
other animals
live and survive
in the harsh world
of the poles.

RED-THROATED LOON

In spring, the red-throated loon migrates to the lakes and tundra of the Arctic. To migrate means to follow the seasons by traveling from one area to another. The red-throated loon flies to the tundra to breed.

SWEEPING FLIGHT
The red-throated loon runs across the surface of the water, then launches itself into the air. It flies with great sweeps of its wings. After nesting in the Arctic, it flies south for the winter.

DIVING FLIPPERS
The red-throated loon is a waterbird and a diver. It has strong, webbed feet.

COURTING DANCE
Red-throated loons have a mating ritual. Together the male and female perform a zig-zag run and a slow race. The male chooses a hollow in the ground close to the water of a tundra pool or lake. Both birds collect twigs and reeds, and heap them into the hollow. After the female lays her eggs, both loons face the water as they sit on them.

SWIMMING CHICKS
The female red-throated loon lays only two eggs. They hatch after about 28 days. New chicks head straight for the water. They can feed themselves 50 days after birth.

FOOD UNDERWATER
Adult red-throated loons cannot walk on land. They are superb divers, however, and live on a diet of fish, shrimp, and crayfish. They also eat frogs.

POLAR BEAR

People have found signs of polar bears almost all the way to the North Pole. These animals are perfectly suited to life in the cold Arctic climate. They have a thick layer of body fat to keep them warm and help them stay afloat in water. In their search for food, they travel very far without tiring. To sleep, they scoop a hollow in the snow, then curl up in this icy "bed."

SNOW FEET
Thick fur grows around the pads of the polar bear's paws. This fur keeps its paws warm. It also gives the bear a soft, silent footfall. The pads are rough and pitted so the bear does not slip on the smooth ice.

THE BIG CATCH
Polar bears tackle beluga whales stranded among the icefloes. The bear springs on the whale's back. With its long claws, it rips the whale's flesh, then hauls the body onto the ice to eat it.

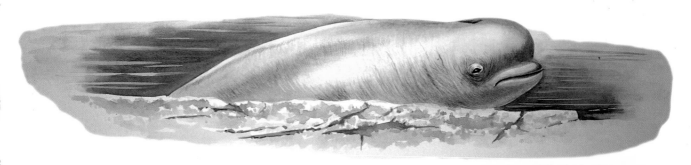

A MEAL UNDER ICE

A polar bear can smell a seal cub even when it is under thick ice. The bear throws its heavy body down to crack the ice open. The bear dives in, and with its sharp teeth, snatches up the cub.

Some male polar bears are ten feet tall (three meters) when they stand up, and weigh over 800 pounds (360 kilograms). Their paws measure one foot (30 centimeters) across. When polar bears swim, they paddle with their front paws. They let their back limbs dangle, or hold them together to help steer. Their thick, white fur is waterproof and is also good camouflage in the snow.

FOOD SMELLS
Polar bears eat plants, berries, fish, and any meat. They can pick up food smells from 15 miles (24 kilometers) away.

A BIG BELLY
The stomach of a polar bear can stretch to carry over 200 pounds (90 kilograms) of food. The bear needs to eat huge meals when it can because food is scarce in the Arctic.

SOFT PRINTS
The polar bear's tracks do not show its claws. Thick fur and well padded paws lift them above the snow.

SNUG IN SNOW

The female builds a den when she is pregnant. She digs it in a snowdrift. She builds where the wind blows down the slope and hides the entrance with snow. The den is about seven feet (two meters) wide and three feet (0.9 meters) high. She moves into the den in October, and gives birth in midwinter.

RICH DIET

Newborn polar bears weigh about one pound (0.5 kilograms). Their mother's milk is rich and nourishing, and the cubs grow very quickly on this diet.

SPRING OUTING

In spring, the mother leaves the den where she has lived for seven months. She is very hungry. She eats plants such as moss before she looks for meat. The cubs follow her and begin to learn about living and hunting in the snow.

ARCTIC WOLF

Arctic wolves live in groups called packs. A pack's leaders are a male and a female known as the "alpha" pair. They are the only pair in the pack that breeds. Most wolves spend their lives in one pack and are loyal to its leaders. Sometimes a young wolf tries to replace the alpha male or leaves to start his own pack.

COMPLETE MEAL
Wolves are omnivorous. This means they eat plants and meat. They eat every part of their prey—bones, skin, fur, and flesh. When meat is scarce, wolves will eat buds and lichen.

TALK AND TRAVEL
Wolves are nocturnal, which means they hunt at night. Their eyesight is poor, but they are guided by a strong sense of smell and sharp hearing. They "talk" to each other with yelps, barks, and whines. At most times, wolves avoid other animals.

RUN AND DIG
Wolves move swiftly with their long legs. Their paws have large claws that help dig holes to bury food.

WORKING TOGETHER
Pack wolves lift their head to howl, and then go hunting. The alpha male leads. The others follow in single file, stepping in his footprints. A few then run ahead to scare the prey. The rest creep up and attack it from behind. They eat the prey as soon as they have brought it down.

FOOD FOR CUBS
Wolves regurgitate, or throw up, some of their food to feed their cubs.

SEAL

Many kinds of seals live in the polar regions. They spend most of their life in the icy water. Seals have a layer of blubber beneath their skin. This fat keeps heat from leaving their body and stops cold from coming in. Like all mammals, seals breathe oxygen from the air and hold it in their blood. Seals have more blood than other mammals, so large amounts of oxygen can be held in the seal's body while it swims underwater.

NETS OF TEETH

The teeth of the leopard seal are strong and sharp. These teeth close to form a mesh like a fishing net. The leopard seal uses them to catch and hold its prey.

HOMELANDS

Leopard seals are found in the freezing waters of the Antarctic. The crabeater seal and the elephant seal also live in these icy southern seas. The common and ringed seals inhabit the northern Arctic regions. The ringed seal's greatest enemy is the polar bear, who hunts it and its pups.

PREPARING A MEAL

Leopard seals hunt penguins and crabeater seals. When it catches a penguin, a leopard seal bites it many times. It shakes the penguin's body in the water. This strips off the penguin's feathers and skin. The seal eats the flesh. The skin is also removed from crabeater seals before they are eaten.

A SECRET NURSERY

Most seals give birth on rocky or icy shelves. A mother ringed seal finds ridges in the sea ice. She digs upwards through these ridges to make a lair beneath the snow. Here her cubs usually are protected from wind and enemies.

Elephant seals have very short limbs. These limbs cannot carry the great weight of their bodies, so on land, elephant seals crawl along on their chest and stomach. They do not look so clumsy while swimming in the sea. They tuck their front limbs against their sides and use their back limbs as flippers to paddle through the water.

BIG DIVER

The male elephant seal grows to a length of sixteen feet (five meters). It weighs over 5,000 pounds (2,250 kilograms). Despite their size, elephant seals can dive swiftly and smoothly to depths of 3,000 feet (900 meters).

NOISY SQUABBLES

During the breeding season, male elephant seals scream, roar, and fight each other over the females.

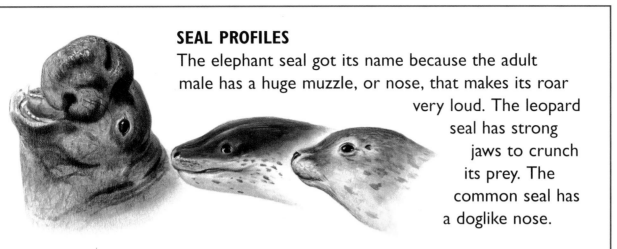

SEAL PROFILES

The elephant seal got its name because the adult male has a huge muzzle, or nose, that makes its roar very loud. The leopard seal has strong jaws to crunch its prey. The common seal has a doglike nose.

ELEPHANT SEAL   **LEOPARD SEAL**   **COMMON SEAL**

KEEPING WARM

Seals stay ashore only to breed, bear young, or moult. Moulting means they shed their outer layer of skin and renew their coat of hair. During moulting, adult elephant seals huddle together, one on top of the other to keep each other warm. On the island of South Georgia, near Antarctica, they may move inland to shallow streams. Here, they lie in the warmth of deep mud.

17

RUFF

In spring, ruffs arrive in the warm, marshy areas of the Arctic tundra. This is where they breed. In this season, the tundra is rich with insects. Ruffs are insectivores, which means they eat insects. The females need a good supply of food for breeding. All ruffs, however, have to fatten up in summer in order to survive their long journey south when the Arctic winter sets in.

A LONG FLIGHT
The ruff is a very strong flier. It has long, wide wings. When it is flying, you can see white oval marks on the sides of its tail. When they leave the tundra, ruffs fly in flocks to warmer parts of Africa, Asia and Europe. Some ruffs travel as far as South Africa.

A WADER
The ruff is a shorebird. It can swim, but does not dive for its food. It wades in the water and uses its long beak to find food.

FEMALES ONLY
The female ruff nests among reeds in a hollow in the ground. She incubates her four eggs by herself. They hatch after 21 days. The chicks can feed themselves soon after birth.

GROUP CHATS

Ruffs are communal, which means that they live in groups. They call to each other with shrill cries and whistles.

LOOK-A-LIKE

In winter, the male ruff has the same brown and white plumage as the female. "Plumage" is the word to describe the feathers of a bird.

PUTTING ON THE RUFF

For their mating ritual, male ruffs grow wonderful plumage. Each grows a "ruff" around its neck with its own pattern of black, brown, cream, and white feathers. The birds gather together in one area, called the "lek." Here they leap, flap, and strut about. The females wander quietly around this display.

PENGUIN

Penguins are suited to life on the shores of Antarctica. They cannot fly. Their wings are stiff flippers used for swimming. Their feet are webbed. Their waterproof feathers are short and smooth. Under their skin, a layer of fat keeps out the cold.

FOOT PROPS
Penguins' feet are set wide apart. These birds lean back on their heels and tails when they stand.

FOOT WARMER

Emperor penguins do not nest. The males hold the egg on their feet. Chicks hatch after 60 days.

GATHERED TOGETHER

There are sixteen species of penguin, and most live on cold, Antarctic shores. On the facing page, jackass penguins gather behind a large emperor penguin. A small yellow-eyed penguin stands nearby. On this page, another emperor stands amongst a group of adélie penguins.

Norman Arlott.

Penguins eat shellfish, squid, and fish. They often spend all day hunting in the sea. When they are caring for their egg, male emperor penguins are too busy to hunt. All the males huddle together for warmth and go without food for about 60 days. After hatching, the chicks are tended by the females. The females leave their chicks with other young and return to feed them once every three or four days.

FINE DISPLAYS

All male penguins give an "ecstatic" display. They lift their heads and flap their wings. They hoot loudly. The display is part of the mating ritual. It is also used to warn others away.

DIVING FORCE

Penguins dive with great force and speed. They may fly through the air for about a yard (0.9 meters) before they enter the water. They store large amounts of oxygen in their blood so they do not have to come up often for air. Some penguins, while hunting food, dive over 100 times a day.

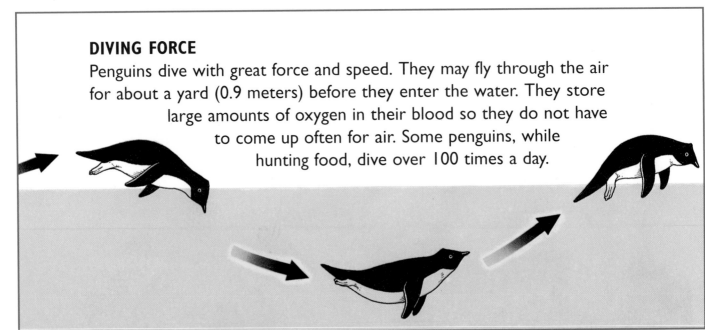

CROWDED NEIGHBORHOOD

Penguins live in colonies made up of thousands of penguins that gather in one place to breed and hunt. A colony of big emperor penguins can cover huge areas of the icy Antarctic.

MANY VOICES

Penguins are very sociable. They greet each other and "talk." Yellow-eyed penguins trumpet. Blue penguins meow like a pet cat, and they also scream loudly. King penguins squawk, trumpet, and whistle.

Norman Arlott

WOLVERINE

Wolverines roam the tundra all around the North Pole. They live alone. In April, a male tracks a female by her scent. About nine months after mating, she gives birth to three or four kits. She tends them by herself in a cave or a den dug into the snow.

GROWLS AND SNARLS
The wolverine has a deep growl and a snarl that frightens most animals. A pack of wolves, however, will attack a wolverine.

STURDY SOLE

The wolverine's feet are slightly webbed and very broad. The width stops them from sinking in snow. Thick hair covers the sole.

A WOLVERINE DIET
Wolverines eat berries, nuts, and meat from the animals shown here. They hunt, but they also scavenge for scraps of prey killed by other animals.

ARCTIC FOX   **ARCTIC HARE**   **SNOW GOOSE**   **MUSK OX CALF**

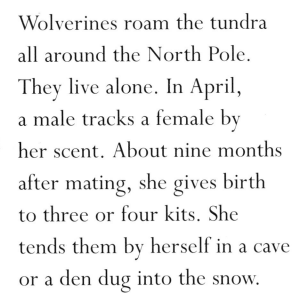

HAPPY ALONE

Wolverines are not friendly. If two meet, they snarl at one another. A female will be aggressive even to males wishing to breed.

SNOWY OWL

Snowy owls are found closer to the North Pole than any other bird. Many stay in the Arctic circle year-round. Some are found farther south. During winter, they live near open places such as fields and prairies. Snowy owls are birds of prey, which means they hunt other animals. They eat gulls, ducks, lemmings, and buntings. They are big and measure almost two feet (60 centimeters) from head to tail.

FLYING HUNTER
Snowy owls perch on rocks or trees. Their sharp eyes scan the tundra for food. Then they swoop down and, while still in flight, catch their prey. Snowy owls also hunt the shallow seas for fish and invertebrates, or boneless creatures, such as squid.

ALL OR NOTHING
A female snowy owl lays between four and fifteen eggs. She sits on the eggs, which hatch in about 30 days. If food is scarce, females do not lay eggs.

THICK FEET
A snowy owl has thick, rough footpads. When the bird lands on freezing surfaces, its footpads do not feel the cold.

STRONG WEAPONS

Snowy owls use their bills and talons, or claws, to hunt and to tear at their food.

COLD HOMES

The snowy owl makes its nest in very cold parts of the tundra. A female looks for hollows in the ground in which to lay her eggs. At birth, the young are weak and helpless. Their parents bring food to them. At the edge of the nest, the father arranges a catch, called a "cache," of lemmings, placed so the chicks can peck at them. They learn to fly at about nine weeks of age.

RIGHT WHALE

Right whales got their name from hunters. For them, these whales were "right" to hunt because they were easy to catch. Right whales are not hunted anymore. In summer, they live in polar waters. There the days are long, and there is plenty of food. In winter, they migrate to the northern parts of the Atlantic and Pacific Oceans to breed.

NETTING THE FOOD
Right whales have baleen plates, or fringes that hang from their upper jaw. The whale travels with its mouth open. It filters plankton from the sea through the fringes.

A BUMPY NOSE
The right whale is also called the Biscay whale. It has growths, called callosities, on the front of its head. Barnacles and sea worms cling to the callosities. Right whales are easy to recognize because of the bumps and barnacles that mark their heads.

RIGHT WHALE DIET

Right whales roam the oceans eating plankton, or tiny sea animals. Sometimes these whales stand on their head to eat shellfish off the sea bed.

OCEAN SONG

Bowhead right whales sing to each other by making a trumpeting sound. They also have a growly purr. A few other whales also sing. No one knows what their sounds mean.

LITTLE ONE

The pygmy above is smaller than other right whales. It has a dorsal fin on its back. Other right whales do not have a dorsal fin.

MUSK OX

Musk oxen live in the
cold Arctic year-round.
They eat willow and sedge,
a kind of grass that grows
on the tundra. Food is
scarce, so musk oxen do
not waste their energy.
They rest for long periods
between feeding.

HEAVY SECURITY

Musk oxen measure eight feet
(2.4 meters) from nose to tail and weigh
over 800 pounds (360 kilograms). Wolves
prefer to attack a young, old,
or crippled musk ox because the healthy
animals are so strong.

HARD TOES

The musk ox is an ungulate.
This means its feet have
hoofs, but no toes or claws.

TOUGH AND QUICK
The musk ox has tough hoofs. It can gallop at 25 miles per hour (40 kilometers per hour).

ALL TOGETHER
Musk oxen live in herds or big groups. They look after each other when they are attacked. The adults form a circle with their horns facing out against the enemy. The calves are gathered inside the circle. If a calf is threatened, an adult will stand between the young and the hunter.

INDEX

GLOSSARY

Carnivore - An animal that eats mainly meat

Camouflage - Many animals have a coat or skin that blends with the color of the place where they live. This is called camouflage. Camouflage hides an animal from predators, or from prey it is trying to catch.

Colony - A large group of animals of the same kind living together is often called a colony. They build their homes in one shared place.

Migrate - Animals migrate when they travel long distances to food, warmth, or to breed.

Moult - Animals moult when they shed their skins, fur, or feathers. Usually, moulting is followed by new growth.

Omnivorous - An animal that eats meat, plants, and insects

Plumage - The feathers covering a bird

Scavenger - An animal that eats what other animals have killed

Tundra - A vast, flat area in the Arctic region. It is treeless, but grass and moss grow there.

Ungulate – An animal that has hoofs